Editor
Eric Migliaccio

Editor in Chief
Karen J. Goldfluss, M.S. Ed.

Creative Director
Sarah M. Smith

Cover Artist
Barb Lorseyedi

Art Coordinator
Renée Mc Elwee

Illustrator
Clint McKnight

Imaging
James Edward Grace

Publisher
Mary D. Smith, M.S. Ed.

NONFICTION Reading Comprehension for the Common Core

TCR 3829

CORRELATED TO COMMON CORE STANDARDS

- Leveled questions that encourage more in-depth thinking skills
- Nonfiction and informational content-area passages
- Student-generated questions and writing activities to extend text comprehension
- Connections to Common Core Informational Text Standards, Foundational Skills, and Language Standards

Teacher Created Resources

Author
Heather Wolpert-Gawron

CORRELATED TO COMMON CORE STANDARDS

For correlations to Common Core State Standards, see page 8 of this book or visit *http://www.teachercreated.com/standards/*.

Teacher Created Resources

6421 Industry Way
Westminster, CA 92683
www.teachercreated.com

ISBN: 978-1-4206-3829-5

© 2014 Teacher Created Resources
Made in U.S.A.

Teacher Created Resources

Table of Contents

Introduction

Reading and comprehending nonfiction or informational text is a challenge. Not everyone can do it well, and it needs to be specifically taught. Students who are great at reading narratives like *Lord of the Rings* or *The Princess Diaries* may still quiver at the possibility of having to understand instructions on uploading an assignment to DropBox. Students who love reading historical fiction may be fearful of reading history. Students who, with flashlight in hand, hide beneath their sheets reading the end of a science-fiction book may glaze over at the sight of an actual factual science article.

Nevertheless, informational text is all around us, and reading it well just takes working out a certain muscle — an informational-text muscle, if you will.

This book is meant to be an informational-muscle gym. Each activity is meant to build in complexity, and each activity is meant to push students in both their reading and their ability to display what they understand about what they read.

In addition to a practice passage, there are 18 reading selections contained in this book. The selections are separated into units, based on their subject matter. As a result, no matter the content area you teach, you will find applicable selections here on which your students can practice.

It doesn't matter what state you teach in, what grade level you teach, or what subject you teach; this book will aid students in understanding more deeply the difficult task of reading informational and nonfiction texts.

Reading Comprehension and the Common Core

The Common Core Standards are here, and with them come a different way to think about reading comprehension. In the past, reading informational text had been compartmentalized, each piece an isolated activity. The Common Core way of thinking is slightly different.

The goal is for students to read different genres and selections of text, pull them together in their heads, and be able to derive a theme or topic that may be shared by them all. In other words, a student may be given three different texts from three different points of view or three different genre standpoints and then have to think about their own thoughts on the subject.

Perhaps a student looks at the following:

1. Instructions on downloading an image from a digital camera
2. A biography about a famous photographer
3. A Google search history on the invention of the camera from the past to the present

Then, from those pieces, the student must pull a common theme or opinion on the topic.

Introduction *(cont.)*

Reading Comprehension and the Common Core *(cont.)*

But to be able to synthesize text (put the thoughts together), a student must first be able to read individual texts and analyze them (pull them apart). That's where this series of books comes in.

Nonfiction Reading Comprehension for the Common Core helps students to hone in on a specific piece of text, identify what's the most important concept in that piece, and answer questions about that specific selection. This will train your students for the bigger challenge that will come later in their schooling: viewing multiple texts and shaking out the meaning of them all.

If you are a public-school teacher, you may be in a state that has adopted the Common Core Standards. Use the selections in this book as individual reading-comprehension activities or pair them with similarly themed selections from other genres to give students a sense of how they will have to pull understanding from the informational, text-heavy world around us.

Copy the individual worksheets as is; or, if you are looking for a more Common Core-aligned format, mimic the Common Core multiple-choice assessments that are coming our way by entering the questions into websites that can help create computer adaptive tests (CATs).

CATs are assessments that allow a student to answer a question, which, depending on whether they answered it correctly or not, leads them to the next question that may be more geared to his or her level. In other words, each student will be taking a differentiated assessment that will end up indicating if a student is capable of answering "Novice" questions up to "Expert" questions.

There are many websites out there that can help you develop assessments to mimic those planned. Create the quiz and embed it into your class webpage or document:

Here are just a couple:

- *http://www.gotoquiz.com/create.html*
- *http://www.quibblo.com/*

Use the selections from this book, and then enter the corresponding questions into the quiz generators. We have identified questions that are higher or lower in level by assigning them a "weight" (from single-weight up through triple-weight). This weight system provides a glimpse of how hard a student should work in order to answer the question correctly. (For more information, read "Leveled Questions" on page 5.)

Regardless of how you choose to use this book, introducing students to the informational world at large is an important way to help them build skills that they will use throughout their schooling and beyond.

Introduction *(cont.)*

Leveled Questions

As you go through this book, you will notice that each question that students will be answering is labeled with icons that look like weights. These icons represent different levels of difficulty. The levels are based on Costa's Levels of Questioning.

The questions in this book are divided into three levels:

Level 1	Level 2	Level 3

These include sentence stems that ask students to . . .	*These include sentence stems that ask students to . . .*	*These include sentence stems that ask students to . . .*
Recite **Define** **Describe** **List**	**Infer** **Compare/Contrast** **Sequence** **Categorize**	**Judge** **Evaluate** **Create** **Hypothesize** **Predict**

The icons are a visual way to make these levels clear to students. That is important because students need to be able to recognize that some questions may require more effort and thought to answer.

Now, most of the multiple-choice questions in this book happen to fall into the Level 1 and Level 2 categories. That is pretty standard for multiple-choice questions. After all, how can asking to create something be defined by an A, B, C, or D answer? However, we may have found a way around that.

At the end of each worksheet is a place for students to develop their own questions about the material they have just read. This brings in a deeper-thinking opportunity. Having your students ask higher-level questions is a great way for assessing their comprehension of what they have read. The deeper the student's question, the deeper his or her understanding of the material.

A student handout called "The Questioning Rubric" is provided on page 6. It serves two purposes:

- It gives your students concrete examples of the elements that make up the different levels of questions.

- It gives you, the teacher, a way to determine whether a student-generated question is a low- or high-level inquiry.

The goal of a student is to ask more challenging questions of oneself. The goal of the teacher is to be able to track better the level of production for each student. This book helps do both.

Introduction *(cont.)*

The Questioning Rubric

Answering questions is one way of proving you understand a reading selection. However, creating your very own questions about the selection might be an even better way. Developing thoughtful, high-level questions can really display your understanding of what you have read, and it also makes other students think about the reading passage in a unique way.

So what types of questions can you ask? There are three levels of questions, and for each one there is a different amount of work your brain must do to answer the question. We've chosen to use a symbol of a weight in order to represent this amount. Consult this chart when thinking about what defines a great question as compared to a so-so one.

Icon	Description
	A single weight represents a **Level 1** question that doesn't require much brainpower to answer correctly. The question only asks readers to tell what they know about the selection. For example, any inquiry that asks for a simple "Yes or No" or "True or False" response is a Level 1 question.
	A double weight represents a **Level 2** question that requires you to use a little more brain sweat. (Ewww!) This question asks readers to think a little beyond the passage. It may require some analysis, inference, or interpretation. Questions involving comparing/contrasting or sequencing often fall here.
	A **Level 3** question really makes you work for its answer. These questions allow you to show off your knowledge of a topic by asking you to create, wonder, judge, evaluate, and/or apply what you know to what you think. These types of questions are much more open-ended than Level 1 or Level 2 questions.

Don't be scared to sweat a little in answering or developing Level 3 questions. Working out your brain in this way will help prepare you for some heavy lifting later on in life. So as you progress through this book, use this rubric as a resource to make sure your questions are as high-level as possible.

Need help getting started? The following sentence stems will give you ideas about how to create questions for each level.

Level 1
- Write the definition of…
- Describe how _____ is…
- List the details that go into…

Level 2
- What can you infer from _____?
- Compare _____ with _____.
- Contrast _____ with _____.
- Write the steps in sequence from _____.
- Place _____ in the right category.

Level 3
- How would you judge the _____?
- How would you evaluate the _____?
- How can you create a _____?
- Hypothesize what would happen if _____.
- What do you predict will happen in _____?

Introduction  (cont.)

Achievement Graph

As you correct your responses in this book, track how well you improve. Calculate how many answers you got right after each worksheet and mark your progress here based on the number of weights each question was worth. For instance, if you get the first problem correct and it is worth two weights, then write "2" in the first column. Do this for each column and add up your total at the end.

Reading Passage	1	2	3	4	Total
"The Library of Alexandria"					
"The First Passengers"					
"Patterns All Around Us"					
"21st-Century Energy Sources"					
"Sci-Fi Influences Science"					
"At the Same Time in History"					
"Fiction Made From Facts"					
"A Remarkable Find"					
"An Enormous Enigma"					
"Multicultural Holidays"					
"The Man Behind the Movies"					
"Science and Art Combined"					
"His Words Live On"					
"One Hungry Imagination"					
"How to Make Lasagna"					
"Videoconferencing"					
"Growing an Edible Garden"					
"How Your Keyboard Works"					
"How to Craft a Quiz"					

Common Core State Standards

The lessons and activities included in *Nonfiction Reading Comprehension for the Common Core, Grade 7* meet the following Common Core State Standards. (©Copyright 2010. National Governors Association Center for Best Practices and Council of Chief State School Officers. All rights reserved.) For more information about the Common Core State Standards, go to *http://www.corestandards.org/* or visit *http://www.teachercreated.com/standards/*.

Informational Text Standards	
Craft and Structure	**Pages**
CCSS.ELA.RI.7.4. Determine the meaning of words and phrases as they are used in a text, including figurative, connotative, and technical meanings.	10–47
Range of Reading and Level of Text Complexity	**Pages**
CCSS.ELA.RI.7.10. By the end of the year, read and comprehend literary nonfiction in the grades 6–8 text complexity band proficiently, with scaffolding as needed at the high end of the range.	10–47
Language Standards	
Conventions of Standard English	**Pages**
CCSS.ELA.L.7.1. Demonstrate command of the conventions of standard English grammar and usage when writing or speaking.	11–47
CCSS.ELA.L.7.2. Demonstrate command of the conventions of standard English capitalization, punctuation, and spelling when writing.	11–47
Knowledge of Language	**Pages**
CCSS.ELA.L.7.3. Use knowledge of language and its conventions when writing, speaking, reading, or listening.	10–47
Vocabulary Acquisition and Use	**Pages**
CCSS.ELA.L.7.4. Determine or clarify the meaning of unknown and multiple-meaning words and phrases based on *grade 7 reading and content*, choosing flexibly from a range of strategies.	10–47
CCSS.ELA.L.7.5. Demonstrate understanding of figurative language, word relationships, and nuances in word meanings.	10–47
CCSS.ELA.L.7.6. Acquire and use accurately grade-appropriate general academic and domain-specific words and phrases; gather vocabulary knowledge when considering a word or phrase important to comprehension or expression.	10–47
Writing Standards	
Production and Distribution of Writing	**Pages**
CCSS.ELA.W.7.4. Produce clear and coherent writing in which the development, organization, and style are appropriate to task, purpose, and audience.	10–47
Research to Build and Present Knowledge	**Pages**
CCSS.ELA.W.7.9. Draw evidence from literary or informational texts to support analysis, reflection, and research.	10–47

Multiple-Choice Test-Taking Tips

Some multiple-choice questions are straightforward and easy. "I know the answer!" your brain yells right away. Some questions, however, stump even the most prepared student. In cases like that, you have to make an educated guess. An educated guess is a guess that uses what you know to help guide your attempt. You don't put your hand over your eyes and pick a random letter! You select it because you've thought about the format of the question, the word choice, the other possible answers, and the language of what's being asked. By making an educated guess, you're increasing your chances of guessing correctly. Whenever you are taking a multiple-choice assessment, you should remember to follow the rules below:

1. Read the directions. It's crucial. You may assume you know what is being asked, but sometimes directions can be tricky when you least expect them to be.

2. Read the questions before you read the passage. Doing this allows you to read the text through a more educated and focused lens. For example, if you know that you will be asked to identify the main idea, you can be on the lookout for that ahead of time.

3. Don't skip a question. Instead, try to make an educated guess. That starts with crossing off the ones you definitely know are not the correct answer. For instance, if you have four possible answers (A, B, C, D) and you can cross off two of them immediately, you've doubled your chances of guessing correctly. If you don't cross off any obvious ones, you would only have a 25% chance of guessing right. However, if you cross off two, you now have a 50% chance!

4. Read carefully for words like *always*, *never*, *not*, *except*, and *every*. Words like these are there to make you stumble. They make the question very specific. Sometimes an answer can be right some of the time, but if a word like *always* or *every* is in the question, the answer must be right *all of the time*.

5. After reading a question, try to come up with the answer first in your head before looking at the possible answers. That way, you will be less likely to bubble or click something you aren't sure about.

6. In questions with an "All of the Above" answer, think of it this way: if you can identify at least two that are correct, then "All of the Above" is probably the correct answer.

7. In questions with a "None of the Above" answer, think of it this way: if you can identify at least two that are *not* correct, then "None of the Above" is probably the correct answer.

8. Don't keep changing your answer. Unless you are sure you made a mistake, usually the first answer you chose is the right one.

The Library of Alexandria

Just imagine a library that contains every book ever written. That was the goal of the rulers who built the Library of Alexandria in Egypt. This great building was imagined and built either during the reign of Ptolemy I or his son, Ptolemy II. It is not known for sure when it was constructed, but it is known that the Library played an important role in Egyptian culture during that era.

The library was huge. It had to be, since it was designed to be a collection of all the world's stories, philosophies, theories, and knowledge! Scholars believe it probably looked a lot like a college or university of today. They believe it included gardens, a dining area, meeting rooms, lecture halls, and lots of books and scrolls. In fact, the local port had a rule that any book on any ship coming into port had to be left for copying. The original would be returned to its owner only after the library had a duplicate. Egypt even sent out people to book fairs beyond its own lands. They found books in places like Athens and Rhodes, and they brought them back to the library. What *foresight* the Egyptians had! They realized how important it would be to have such a collection, and they put the steps in place to create the most unique library ever assembled.

Unfortunately, it was not to last. Historians believe that during the Roman Conquest, Julius Caesar set fire to the library. He may even have done this by accident. The building, and all it contained, was lost forever. Still, the legend that it left behind helps to fuel future dreams. In fact, a similar library is now being "built." Its goal is to collect all the books ever printed and provide them in one online library. It's a new Library of Alexandria for a new century.

Answer the following questions about the story "The Library of Alexandria." The weights show you how hard you will need to work to find each answer.

1. What was the purpose of the Library of Alexandria?

    Ⓐ to collect all the stories known to man

    Ⓑ to learn about other cultures, philosophies, and theories

    Ⓒ to gather as much knowledge as possible

    Ⓓ all of the above

2. Based on the passage, what can you infer is meant by "having foresight"?

    Ⓐ thinking ahead   Ⓒ being unsure

    Ⓑ being excited   Ⓓ thinking creatively

3. Who possibly destroyed the Library of Alexandria?

    Ⓐ Cleopatra   Ⓒ Ptolemy II

    Ⓑ Ptolemy I   Ⓓ Julius Caesar

4. Why don't we know for sure what the library looked like?

    Ⓐ It was too big to see all of it.   Ⓒ It was all moved online.

    Ⓑ It was burned down.   Ⓓ It was sold in book fairs.

On the lines below, write your own question based on "The Library of Alexandria." Circle the correct picture on the left to show the level of the question you wrote.

_____

_____

_____

_____

On a separate piece of paper . . .

- Write a sentence that includes the word *assembled*.

- Have you ever lost something that was priceless? Something that is priceless has so much value that no money in the world could buy it again. What happened, and how did you feel?

The First Passengers

About 130,000 spectators, including King Louis XVI, looked up into the sky above France and saw a large balloon soaring overhead. The balloon was filled with hot air. It had a basket attached to the bottom of it. The basket held the first passengers ever to fly in a hot-air balloon. The day was September 19, 1783. After eight minutes and two miles of flight, the balloon landed. All of the passengers got off safely. Who were the passengers? They were a sheep, a duck, and a rooster.

Only a year before, two men filled a silk and paper bag with hot air and watched as it rose up to the ceiling of a house. Since the hot air was less dense than the air around it, it could rise. These men, who were brothers, started experimenting with bigger and bigger bags. It was they who, under advice from the king, launched the farm animals into the sky on that September day in 1783.

The early balloon looked a little different than the hot-air balloons do of today. For one thing, it was highly decorated to impress the French royalty in the crowd.

Only two months later, the first humans flew in a hot-air balloon. It took a lot of bravery because it was still a very young science. The first man to fly in a balloon was a chemistry and physics teacher. He just went straight up and then straight back down. Why? His balloon was tethered to the ground with a rope. Soon, another man tried an untethered flight. He landed his balloon about five miles away from his starting point. From that point on, people began flying further and further.

Jean-Pierre Blanchard was another pioneer in the history of balloon flight. Not only that, he was also the first to use another important invention. When faced with an emergency situation, Blanchard used a parachute to successfully jump out of a balloon in mid-flight.

Answer the following questions about the story "The First Passengers." The weights show you how hard you will need to work to find each answer.

1. What was the occupation of the first man to fly in a balloon?

Ⓐ king

Ⓑ teacher

Ⓒ inventor

Ⓓ passenger

2. What made the first balloon rise?

Ⓐ hot air

Ⓑ cold air

Ⓒ ice

Ⓓ silk

3. The title of the passage is "The First Passengers." To whom does this title refer?

Ⓐ King Louis XVI

Ⓑ Jean-Pierre Blanchard

Ⓒ French royalty

Ⓓ three animals

4. Based on the passage, what does the word *tethered* mean?

Ⓐ let go

Ⓑ cut off

Ⓒ tied to

Ⓓ blown away

On the lines below, write your own question based on "The First Passengers." Circle the correct picture on the left to show the level of the question you wrote.

_____

_____

_____

_____

___

On a separate piece of paper . . .

- Write a sentence that includes the word *invention*.

- The first balloon that flew for the king had symbols on it that represented him. If you were designing a balloon, what symbols would you put on it to represent you? Draw your balloon, complete with symbols on the bag.

Patterns All Around Us

Have you ever looked really closely at the leaf on a fern? If you did, you'd see that it almost looks as if the leaf of the fern is made up of smaller versions of itself. That is, it looks like the shape of each fern leaf is made up of many fern-leaf shapes. And if you looked even closer, those smaller fern-leaf shapes look as if they're made up of even smaller fern-leaf shapes. This is repeated again and again, with each set of shapes being smaller and smaller. There must be a name for this amazing kind of pattern, right? There is. The shape of the fern leaf represents what is called a *fractal*.

A mathematician named Benoit Mandelbrot first identified fractals. He gave them their name in 1975. He also proposed that larger shapes, like coastlines or clouds, may seem to be random and chaotic but really represent repeating shapes. He used fractal math to prove his theories and even began creating pictures of fractals using a computer. If you go online and search for "Fractals Images," you'll see many of those that Mandelbrot created.

Fractals are intricate, repeating shapes that can be mathematically proven. It's true: while these fascinating fractals may look like art, they are really a form of math. They are a form of geometry. In geometry, you study the shapes that make up our world. The prefix *geo-* relates to Earth, while -*metry* relates to measurement. As you already know, there are many geometric shapes in nature. There are squares, circles, rectangles, etc. However, a fractal is another kind of shape, albeit one that is far more complex. With this complexity can come great beauty.

A snowflake is a great example of a fractal. It is composed of repeating shapes that are too small to see with the naked eye. Together, these many small shapes form a bigger shape that is large enough for us to see without the aid of a microscope or other instrument.

Answer the following questions about the story "Patterns All Around Us." The weights show you how hard you will need to work to find each answer.

1. Who gave fractals their name?

- Ⓐ Mandelbrot
- Ⓑ Mozart
- Ⓒ Newton
- Ⓓ Euclid

2. Based on the passage, what does a geologist study?

- Ⓐ math
- Ⓑ earth
- Ⓒ sky
- Ⓓ shapes

3. Based on the passage, what can you infer is the meaning of the phrase "the naked eye?"

- Ⓐ a face without glasses
- Ⓑ an eye without clothing
- Ⓒ what the eye can see by itself without aid
- Ⓓ what can be seen with a microscope

4. Which of these words from the passage *best* describes fractals?

- Ⓐ "random"
- Ⓑ "chaotic"
- Ⓒ "repeating"
- Ⓓ "fern-like"

On the lines below, write your own question based on "Patterns All Around Us." Circle the correct picture on the left to show the level of the question you wrote.

_____

_____

_____

_____

___

On a separate piece of paper . . .

- Write a sentence that includes the word *complex*.
- What are some other fractals in nature that you can think of?

___

21st-Century Energy Sources

We use energy to help fuel almost everything we do. We can see in the dark using electricity. We can keep cool in the summer by simply turning on our air conditioner or our electric fans. We can travel far and wide as long as we have enough gasoline for our cars or fuel for our planes. We have used the same kinds of fuels for many years, and we live in a time when there are many more options than ever before. The question, however, is if some of our energy sources will be around in the future.

There are two kinds of energy: renewable and nonrenewable. If something is nonrenewable, it goes away once it's used. Think of a candle as an example of a nonrenewable energy source. Once you set the wick on fire, the candle begins to burn down. Eventually, it will burn completely out and then it will be gone forever. If an energy source is renewable, then to the best of our knowledge, that means the energy source will continue to be available even if we use it. These energy sources make more of themselves. They renew themselves.

Some examples of nonrenewable energy include coal, natural gas, and petroleum. Our species has been using them for a long time, and these forms of energy have become very important to us. We could not live the way we do without them. That is why it is so important that we find alternative ways to produce energy. That is why we are learning about other ways to keep our world lit up, running, flying, and cool.

Here are some renewable energy sources:

1. **Solar** – Solar energy comes from the sun. Using special panels, people can gather up energy from the sun to convert sunlight into electricity. To convert something means to change it from one form to another. Some people use solar panels on their homes or in their gardens.

2. **Wind** – Wind energy comes from wind turbines. Turbines look like huge windmills. When the wind spins the propellers, the energy creates electricity that can be used to light entire neighborhoods.

3. **Water** – Hydropower is power created from water. The prefix *hydro* means "water." People have built dams to help create hydropower. When water runs through a dam, the current spins a turbine (which acts like a propeller). That turbine helps to create electricity.

Answer the following questions about the story "21st-Century Energy Sources." The weights show you how hard you will need to work to find each answer.

1. What is an example of nonrenewable energy?

    Ⓐ gas   Ⓒ wind

    Ⓑ solar   Ⓓ water

2. Based on the passage, what can you infer is the meaning of the word *hydrophobic*?

    Ⓐ afraid of flying   Ⓒ afraid of water

    Ⓑ afraid of spiders   Ⓓ afraid of the dark

3. What does the word *convert* mean?

    Ⓐ to teach   Ⓒ to change

    Ⓑ to remain the same   Ⓓ to generate

4. Based on the information given in the story, why should we discover new renewable forms of energy?

    Ⓐ Renewable energy might last longer.

    Ⓑ Renewable energy is louder.

    Ⓒ Nonrenewable energy is expensive.

    Ⓓ Renewable energy is dangerous.

On the lines below, write your own question based on "21st-Century Energy Sources." Circle the correct picture on the left to show the level of the question you wrote.

_____

_____

_____

_____

On a separate piece of paper . . .

- Write a sentence that includes the word *solar*.

- Think ahead to a future time. What resource can you imagine might be discovered to help fuel our world?

Sci-Fi Influences Science

Science is about studying the way our world works. It's also about inventing the amazing things that we want to see in the future. But did you know that a lot of what has become fact started out as fiction? That's right, science fiction. Science fiction is a reading genre (category) that is all about made-up stories that are based in real science. *Star Trek* is science fiction. So are *Star Wars* and *The Hunger Games*. That is, each of these books or movies has real science somewhere in them, but a made-up story has been written around that science.

This relationship between science and science fiction works both ways. In many cases, science had to be influenced by science fiction before it could become true. For instance, without dreaming about flying, writing about flying, and sketching flight, we could never have invented an airplane. In the same way, the dream of breathing underwater led to the invention of the scuba tank. For another example, the inventor of the cell phone credits *Star Trek's* "communicator" device as a major influence.

The list below shows a few items or ideas that first appeared in science fiction, but that now are on the way to becoming real science:

1. **The Flying Car** – We don't know who first thought of the flying car, but the concept has appeared in everything from *The Simpsons* to movies like *Chitty Chitty Bang Bang*. Now, many countries have their own prototypes being developed. A prototype is the first model of something.

2. **The Jet Pack** – The thought of flying people can be traced back for centuries. From *Peter Pan* to *Ironman*, books and movies have long had a fascination with people who could fly. Now, there are many versions of jet packs in development. Some use water to propel a person skyward. Some use powerful thrusters. It doesn't seem the safest invention yet, but scientists are sure working on it!

3. **Colonizing Other Planets** – We don't yet have humans living on other planets, but scientists are thinking about all of the important questions for forming a colony on a distant world. A colony is a group of settlers that explore and live in a new land. Scientists are planning where humans might be able to go, what they would need to survive, and how humans might travel to their new planet. Maybe your grandchildren will have the chance to visit a new world one day!

Answer the following questions about the story "Sci-Fi Influences Science." The weights show you how hard you will need to work to find each answer.

1. Based on how the passage defines *science fiction*, what can you infer is the meaning of *historical fiction*?

   Ⓐ a true story   Ⓒ a fantasy

   Ⓑ a made-up story based in facts   Ⓓ a fairy tale

2. Based on the passage, what is a kind of prototype?

   Ⓐ a final draft of an essay   Ⓒ a first draft of an essay

   Ⓑ the winning science fair project   Ⓓ a 3rd draft of an essay

3. What is an example of something that might be in a science-fiction book?

   Ⓐ a rocket ship to Mars

   Ⓑ an invention to cure worldwide hunger

   Ⓒ a super-speed train that connects the U.S. with Europe

   Ⓓ all of the above

4. Which of these is not mentioned as an example of science fiction?

   Ⓐ *Star Wars*   Ⓒ *The Hunger Games*

   Ⓑ *Star Trek*   Ⓓ *Little House on the Prairie*

On the lines below, write your own question based on "Sci-Fi Influences Science." Circle the correct picture on the left to show the level of the question you wrote.

_____

_____

_____

_____

On a separate piece of paper . . .

- Write a sentence that includes the word *colonize*.

- Think about an invention that you believe needs to exist. Draw a picture of your invention, and label all of its parts.

At the Same Time in History

It's fascinating to think about what was going on in different civilizations around the world at the same time. Let's say that your class is learning about the Gold Rush and about the events that led to the Civil War. These things were happening during the mid-1800s in the United States. Meanwhile, other important events were also taking place at that time on other continents. The word *meanwhile* means "at the same time." For example, you might have been in your bedroom at 7:00 a.m. this morning, getting ready for school. Meanwhile, your little sister was having her bottle in the kitchen.

It can be really interesting to learn what was happening in different parts of the world at the same point in history. So let's do that now. Let's look at the world during the mid-1800s. We'll zoom in like a camera and look at what was happening in different civilizations at the same time.

- **North America** – By 1850, the California Gold Rush was in full swing. It had exploded just two years **prior** when John Marshall discovered gold at Sutter's Mill. Within just a few years, over 300,000 people came to California from all over the world to try their luck in the hunt for gold.

- **Japan** – By the mid-1800s, the era of the samurai was about to end. The samurai were like knights who helped form the Japanese military for centuries. However, towards the middle of the 1800s, U.S. steamships came to the island of Japan to trade and share their ideas. It marked the end of the samurai because the Japanese people were no longer living in isolation, and their ideas began to change when the cultures collided.

- **Europe** – Starting in the mid-1800s, many countries in Europe were at war. The Crimean War lasted from 1853–1856. It included many countries and empires like Russia, Britain, the French and Ottoman Empire. The Crimean War was one of the first wars in which telegraphs were used for communication and photographs were taken to capture the images of battle.

Look at a timeline sometime and ask yourself, "What is happening around the world right now?

Answer the following questions about the story "At the Same Time in History." The weights show you how hard you will need to work to find each answer.

1. Based on the passage, what seems to be the meaning of the word *prior*?

Ⓐ before   Ⓒ through

Ⓑ after   Ⓓ around

2. Based on the passage, what year did the Gold Rush begin?

Ⓐ 1850   Ⓒ 1848

Ⓑ 1856   Ⓓ 1851

3. Which of these countries is not mentioned as having been involved in the Crimean War?

Ⓐ France   Ⓒ Russia

Ⓑ Britain   Ⓓ Kenya

4. Which of these was not a part of Japanese life prior to the mid-1800s?

Ⓐ the era of the samurai

Ⓑ visits from the U.S.

Ⓒ living in isolation

Ⓓ the formation of the military

On the lines below, write your own question based on "At the Same Time in History." Circle the correct picture on the left to show the level of the question you wrote.

_____

_____

_____

_____

On a separate piece of paper . . .

• Write a sentence that includes the word *meanwhile*.

• Go to *http://worldhistoryproject.org/* and pick a date. Find at least five events that happened on that date.

Fiction Made From Facts

A reading genre is a category of book. There are many kinds of reading genres. For starters, here are a few:

- **Fantasy** – This genre might include mythical creatures, dragons, and knights.

- **Young Adult** – In this genre, characters are generally teenagers, and the conflicts focus on the drama of being a teenager.

- **Nonfiction** – Stories that fall under this category should include only facts and information.

- **Poetry** – Examples from this genre might be in the form of odes, limericks, sonnets, or other forms of poetry.

- **Drama** – Plays fall under this category. This type of writing is characterized by dialogue and stage directions.

There is also a genre called "historical fiction." Historical fiction is a very important genre because we not only learn about the characters and stories, we also learn about the history in which the story is set.

The setting in historical fiction is really important. One aspect of the setting in a story is the location and the era in which the story is set. Historical fiction is set in the past, and the author uses facts to help propel the made-up story. Sometimes that means that there are famous people in the story. For instance, a story set during the Civil War might have the main character shake the hand of Abraham Lincoln. Historical-fiction stories might also feature famous events that really took place. For instance, a story set during the London Blitz might have the main character trying to run for a bomb shelter in the middle of the night.

Historical fiction helps teach us about different cultures. It also helps us learn to empathize with people who lived in a different time and place. Feeling empathetic towards a character means that you really feel understanding for what he or she has to go through. By creating characters that readers really care about, writers can teach readers a lot about a time or place that they know nothing about.

Answer the following questions about the story "Fiction Made From Facts." The weights show you how hard you will need to work to find each answer.

1. Which of these is not an example of a reading genre?

   Ⓐ historical fiction   Ⓑ drama   Ⓒ young adult   Ⓓ limericks

2. What of the following are elements of a story's setting?

   Ⓐ the country in which a story takes place   Ⓒ the buildings and locations
   Ⓑ the era in which a story takes place   Ⓓ all of the above

3. Based on the information in the passage, why is reading historical fiction a good thing?

   Ⓐ The characters are more interesting.
   Ⓑ The stories are full of conflicts and solutions.
   Ⓒ The stories take place in the real world.
   Ⓓ The reader learns about situations that he or she may never have experienced.

4. Based on what you know of the definition of "historical fiction," what can you infer is the definition of the reading genre "science fiction"?

   Ⓐ It is a nonfiction genre made up entirely of facts.
   Ⓑ It is a made-up story that uses science like aliens or future worlds to help tell the story.
   Ⓒ It is a story about the history of science.
   Ⓓ It is like a textbook that provides only true information about science.

On the lines below, write your own question based on "Fiction Made From Facts." Circle the correct picture on the left to show the level of the question you wrote.

_____

_____

_____

_____

On a separate piece of paper . . .

- Write a sentence that includes the word *category*.
- What is your favorite reading genre, and why?

A Remarkable Find

For years after they were discovered, archeologists and scientists couldn't figure out what all those pictures on the Egyptian tombs and artwork meant. They couldn't understand the artifacts they found from the ancient Egyptian culture. The symbols on the walls and tombs and vases clearly represented a language, but nobody knew what that language was saying. Until one day, in 1799, a French solider unearthed what became known as the Rosetta Stone.

The Rosetta Stone was a remarkable find. It was a *stele*, a stone slab, on which was carved a single piece of text. What makes the stone so scientifically valuable is that this piece of text is written in three different languages. This was the breakthrough that scientists needed. Knowing what the authors were trying to say, and being able to compare known words with three ancient languages, helped to break the code that became known as the ancient hieroglyphic language. The way it works is this:

Imagine you have a document in a language you understand. Maybe it's a simple letter that starts with "*Dear Peter, please come home for dinner.*" Then, you find that same line written in three different languages.

Spanish: Querido Peter, por favor vuelve a casa para la cena.

French: Cher Peter, s'il vous plaît revenir à la maison pour le dîner.

Italian: Caro Peter, ti aspettiamo a casa per cena.

From looking at all three languages and knowing what the original document said, you can figure out, for example, that "Cher" in French means "Dear" in English. The Rosetta Stone worked much the same way.

Since then, the term "Rosetta Stone" has become an idiom in the English language. An idiom is an expression used to describe something in a culture. In this case, the term "Rosetta Stone" is used to describe the clue that is used to solve a mystery.

Answer the following questions about the story "A Remarkable Find." The weights show you how hard you will need to work to find each answer.

1. Based on what you learned from the passage, what is the Italian word for "Dear?"

 Ⓐ   *Claro*   Ⓒ   *Caro*

 Ⓑ   *Cher*   Ⓓ   *Carus*

2. Which of the following is not an example of an idiom?

 Ⓐ   He is pulling my leg!

 Ⓑ   You should keep an eye out for the lost book.

 Ⓒ   You seem to have a chip on your shoulder.

 Ⓓ   This is a fantastic book!

3. According to the passage, what is a *stele*?

 Ⓐ   a sliver of rock   Ⓒ   a piece of pottery

 Ⓑ   a big chunk of stone   Ⓓ   a tomb

4. How many languages were found carved into the Rosetta Stone?

 Ⓐ   2   Ⓒ   4

 Ⓑ   3   Ⓓ   5

On the lines below, write your own question based on "A Remarkable Find." Circle the correct picture on the left to show the level of the question you wrote.

_____

_____

_____

_____

On a separate piece of paper . . .

- Write a sentence that includes the word *ancient*.

- Are you bilingual? Do you know more than one language? If you do, what are the similarities between English and your other spoken language(s)?

An Enormous Enigma

An enormous enigma sits in a field of grass deep in the English countryside. Something is an enigma if it is a mystery, a puzzle that is difficult to understand or solve. This enigma is a circular structure that is made of massive stones. These ancient stones are nearly 5,000 years old, and some of the largest ones weigh as much 50 tons. Together, the rocks form a monument called Stonehenge. It is one of the most famous sites in the world, attracting about a million visitors each year.

How was Stonehenge built, and who built it? These questions are among the greatest mysteries in history. They still puzzle us to this day. We can only piece together the clues that we have from studying Stonehenge.

With the knowledge we now have, we can determine that Stonehenge was built over a period of about 1,500 years. Construction began in about 3100 BCE and continued over various stages until about 1600 BCE. These were prehistoric times, so we don't have any written record of how or why the monument was built. Scientists can only examine the evidence that they have found. This evidence, however, raises many questions that do not have simple answers:

Why is the monument built from these particular stones? The huge stones that form Stonehenge do not come from the immediate area. They had to be moved over miles of rough terrain to get there.

How were these massive stones moved such long distances? This was before modern equipment. The monument also features several groups of three huge stones — two standing on end with another large stone placed across the top. How could this have been accomplished so long ago?

What was the purpose of Stonehenge? There may be several answers to this question. It may have been used as a kind of observatory, for example. The monument seems to be aligned with the rising of the sun at certain times of the year. Stonehenge has likely also served as a sacred burial site at one time or another. A large number of bones and artifacts have been unearthed in the area.

Will we ever fully uncover the secrets of Stonehenge? For now, the answer to that question remains an enigma, too.

Answer the following questions about the story "An Enormous Enigma." The weights show you how hard you will need to work to find each answer.

1. Based on the passage, what is the definition of *prehistoric*?

   Ⓐ "mysterious"   Ⓒ "very important"

   Ⓑ "made of stone"   Ⓓ "before written records"

2. Which question is not given in the passage as a reason why Stonehenge is mysterious?

   Ⓐ Why were those rocks used?

   Ⓑ How were the rocks moved?

   Ⓒ Why was Stonehenge built?

   Ⓓ Why do so many people visit Stonehenge?

3. Which of these words from the passage does not begin with a prefix?

   Ⓐ uncover   Ⓒ prehistoric

   Ⓑ circular   Ⓓ unearthed

4. An analogy is a comparison of two things. Look at the first part of this analogy to determine what the missing answer should be.

   Stone is to rock as *mystery* is to _____.

   Ⓐ *enormous*   Ⓒ *massive*

   Ⓑ *enigma*   Ⓓ *sacred*

On the lines below, write your own question based on "An Enormous Enigma." Circle the correct picture on the left to show the level of the question you wrote.

_____

_____

_____

_____

On a separate piece of paper . . .

- Write a sentence that includes the word *enormous*.

- Why do you think so many people visit Stonehenge each year? Explain your answer.

Multicultural Holidays

Most Americans know why the United States celebrates the Fourth of July. Many have heard the story of Thanksgiving or of St. Patrick's Day. On the other hand, there are several lesser-known holidays that are celebrated throughout America. The United States has a diverse population, and this results in many holidays that come from different countries, cultures, and faiths.

Here are a few examples:

- **Chinese New Year** – The Chinese New Year is celebrated in many countries with a large Chinese population. The holiday celebrates the gods and the ancestors of the families. People honor this holiday with parades and firecrackers. In addition, many families clean their houses to let in good luck, hang red banners by their doors, and give out gifts of money to the children.

- **Rosh Hashanah** – Rosh Hashanah marks the Jewish New Year. It typically takes place in the fall. Rosh Hashanah is celebrated through dance and through blowing a huge horn called a *shofar*. People eat sweet dishes, like apples dipped in honey. During this time, people say hello to each other by saying, "Shanah Tovah." In Hebrew this means, "Have a good year."

- **Cinco de Mayo** – In Spanish, "Cinco de Mayo" means "the 5th of May." Every May 5, a holiday is celebrated. It is a Mexican holiday that honors the victory of the Mexican Army over the French at the Battle of Puebla. Even though the Mexicans were eventually defeated, the holiday came to symbolize Mexican unity. People celebrate Cinco de Mayo with big parties, mariachi music, and colorful *folklórico* dancing.

All of these holidays are a part of America and its diverse population of people. Now you will have an educated answer to give when someone asks, "Why do we celebrate this holiday?"

Answer the following questions about the story "Multicultural Holidays." The weights show you how hard you will need to work to find each answer.

1. In what season is Rosh Hashanah celebrated?

   Ⓐ winter   Ⓒ summer

   Ⓑ spring   Ⓓ fall

2. What is not mentioned as a way in which the Chinese New Year is celebrated?

   Ⓐ hanging yellow banners   Ⓒ cleaning the houses

   Ⓑ watching parades   Ⓓ gifting money to children

3. The Spanish word for January is *Enero.* Based on what you have read, what would be the meaning of the Spanish phrase "Cinco de Enero"?

   Ⓐ "May 5"   Ⓒ "January holiday"

   Ⓑ "Have a good year."   Ⓓ "January 5"

4. What reason does the story give for why Americans celebrate so many different holidays?

   Ⓐ because America has such a diverse population

   Ⓑ because all Americans like to go to parties

   Ⓒ because all Americans like different foods

   Ⓓ because Americans like to have days off from work

On the lines below, write your own question based on "Multicultural Holidays." Circle the correct picture on the left to show the level of the question you wrote.

_____

_____

_____

_____

On a separate piece of paper . . .

- Write a sentence that includes the word *honor.*

- If you could designate a holiday, what holiday would you create? Who/what would you honor?

The Man Behind the Movies

Did you know that both Luke Skywalker and Indiana Jones came from the mind of the same man? That's right, two of film's most popular characters were created by a man named George Lucas. George Lucas is a writer, director, innovator, and philanthropist. A philanthropist is someone who donates his or her money to helping others or helping with a particular cause.

George Lucas was born in 1944 in a small town in California. He originally wanted to become a racecar driver, despite the dangers of that sport. By the time he attended college, he realized that directing films was his dream. He studied cinematography. The prefix *cine-* means "related to movies and film." The suffix *-graphy* means "the study of." Cinematography is the study of film and how to translate the images in your head to the movie screen.

George began developing ideas and making movies. His first film was released in 1971, and it was not a success. It didn't make much money and not many people saw it. That didn't stop Lucas, however. His next film, *American Graffiti*, was about a group of teenagers. It was made for approximately $780,000, but it went on to make about $50 million! This success allowed Lucas the freedom to make a project that had been sitting in his head for years. It was a story that he claims is like a Western set in outer space. It was a classic story of good versus evil, but it had the most amazing special effects ever seen on film at that time. The movie was called *Star Wars*.

Star Wars has since become its own business. It has multiple sequels as well as toys, TV shows, and books. From the money earned, Lucas went on to create Industrial Light and Magic, a studio that helps other directors create the most current special visual and sound effects. Among his many projects, Lucas went on to develop a series of films built around the very popular Indiana Jones character.

While he is known as a great filmmaker, George pursues many other interests. In fact, one of his greatest passions is education. In the early 1990s, George Lucas started the George Lucas Educational Foundation (GLEF). GLEF's mission is to showcase the wonderful things going on in our schools all around the country. Its website, Edutopia, is named to reflect both its science fiction roots and the hope that all schools can be great. The word part *-utopia* means "a place like no other." Therefore, "Edutopia," means a unique place for education.

Answer the following questions about the story "The Man Behind the Movies." The weights show you how hard you will need to work to find each answer.

1. Based on what you learned from the passage, what can you infer is the definition of the word *filmography*?

Ⓐ taking pictures   Ⓒ the study of films

Ⓑ designing photos   Ⓓ watching movies

2. From its use in the last paragraph, what can you infer is the definition of the word *showcase*?

Ⓐ display in an effective way   Ⓒ reflect what is seen

Ⓑ put in a box for later   Ⓓ create a unique place

3. About how old was George Lucas when his first film was produced?

Ⓐ 36   Ⓒ 27

Ⓑ 37   Ⓓ 46

4. Based on what you learned about George Lucas, which of these words does not give a good description of him?

Ⓐ persistent   Ⓒ inventive

Ⓑ creative   Ⓓ unimaginative

On the lines below, write your own question based on "The Man Behind the Movies." Circle the correct picture on the left to show the level of the question you wrote.

_____

_____

_____

_____

_____

On a separate piece of paper . . .

- Write a sentence that includes the word *showcase*.

- A utopia is a unique and perfect place. In your opinion, what are the characteristics (qualities) of your perfect utopia?

Science and Art Combined

Many of us have seen Leonardo da Vinci's paintings. His works hang in museums all over the world. Perhaps you've heard of the *Mona Lisa*, a painting that is famous for its subject's small smile. Perhaps you've seen pictures of *The Last Supper*, a painting that depicts a moment in the Bible. What's truly fascinating about Leonardo da Vinci, however, is that his talents didn't end with his paintbrush. He was also a man of science.

Using his pencils, he dreamed up and sketched numerous designs, some of which we use today. Four hundred years before the Wright Brothers created their simple airplane, da Vinci invented a helicopter-like vehicle called an ornithopter. The prefix *orni-* means "relating to birds." He also designed a more airplane-like device that he named a flying machine. It had wings more like those of a bird. He developed tanks that he called armor cars. These were vehicles that looked like they were wearing large hats designed to protect them from attack. He even developed an early version of a parachute, as well as a calculator.

Leonardo da Vinci was born in 1452 in Italy. He studied to be an artist, but he grew into perhaps history's most famous "Renaissance man." Nowadays you don't have to be a man to be considered a Renaissance man. The term is used to describe a person who is skilled in many subjects and areas. To da Vinci, his art helped him visualize the science, while the science helped to inform his art. His paintings were so life-like, it was clear that he had studied how bodies really looked, how nature really acted, and how objects really moved.

By his death in 1519, Leonardo da Vinci had studied and contributed to many fields of study, most notably those in engineering (where he learned how machines worked), geology (where he learned about the various components that made up the earth), hydrodynamics (where he learned about how water functioned), mathematics (where he learned about proportions in life), and zoology (where he learned about animals).

Leonardo da Vinci definitely used his brain to learn about the world around him. Then, he painted the world.

Answer the following questions about the story "Science and Art Combined." The weights show you how hard you will need to work to find each answer.

1. About how old was Leonardo da Vinci when he died?

Ⓐ 57

Ⓒ 77

Ⓑ 67

Ⓓ 87

2. To be considered a Renaissance man, what must you be?

Ⓐ male

Ⓒ skilled in many different subjects

Ⓑ born during the Renaissance Era

Ⓓ all of the above

3. Which of the following is not named as a subject that da Vinci studied?

Ⓐ hydrodynamics

Ⓒ engineering

Ⓑ economics

Ⓓ zoology

4. Based on what you learned from the passage, what can you infer is the meaning of the word *ornithology*?

Ⓐ the study of helicopters

Ⓒ the study of tanks

Ⓑ the study of birds

Ⓓ the study of parachutes

On the lines below, write your own question based on "Science and Art Combined." Circle the correct picture on the left to show the level of the question you wrote.

_____

_____

_____

_____

On a separate piece of paper . . .

- Write a sentence that includes the word *nowadays*.

- It's possible that you are also a Renaissance man. Make a bulleted list of subjects you like to study.

His Words Live On

Did you know that many of the words and expressions we use today were actually invented by William Shakespeare? Shakespeare, or The Bard, as he is also known, is one of the greatest writers of all time. Born in England in 1564, Shakespeare wrote about 38 full plays, 154 sonnets, and various other poems. In the course of doing so, Shakespeare invented at least 1,500 words and expressions. Here are some of the words and phrases that came from Shakespeare:

eyeball	*fair play*	*laughingstock*
puking	*full circle*	*Knock knock! Who's there?*
in a pickle	*fashionable*	

So, for example, let's look at the following passage from his play *As You Like It*:

> *All the world's a stage,*
> *And all the men and women merely players;*
> *They have their exits and their entrances,*
> *And one man in his time plays many parts,*
> *His acts being seven ages. At first, the infant,*
> *Mewling and puking in the nurse's arms.*

Here are those same words, translated into the language of today:

> *Life is like the theater,*
> *Everyone is an actor;*
> *They are all born and die,*
> *And everyone has seven chapters in his or her lifetime.*
> *The first stage is the baby,*
> *Crying and puking in his babysitter's arms.*

See? The word *puking* means the same thing today as it did when Shakespeare wrote it, yet it was the first time that word ever appeared in print. His words *transcend* generations. The prefix *trans-* means "across" or "beyond." That is, his words have been read across many years and still mean something to the people of today.

Answer the following questions about the story "His Words Live On." The weights show you how hard you will need to work to find each answer.

1. A sonnet is a type of poem. Based on the story, which answer best names the number of poems Shakespeare wrote?

   Ⓐ   38   Ⓒ   154

   Ⓑ   54   Ⓓ   over 154

2. Based on the context of the passage, what can you infer is the meaning of the phrase "conservative estimate"?

   Ⓐ   wild guess   Ⓒ   exact answer

   Ⓑ   safe guess   Ⓓ   precise number

3. Based on what you learned from the passage, you can predict that a transatlantic flight might do what?

   Ⓐ   fly across the Atlantic Ocean   Ⓒ   fly south for the winter

   Ⓑ   sail around the world   Ⓓ   drive up north

4. Which word was *not* identified as one invented by Shakespeare?

   Ⓐ   fashionable   Ⓒ   eyeball

   Ⓑ   puking   Ⓓ   mewling

On the lines below, write your own question based on "His Words Live On." Circle the correct picture on the left to show the level of the question you wrote.

_____

_____

_____

_____

_____

On a separate piece of paper . . .

- Write a sentence that includes the phrase "in a pickle."

- Have you ever thought to invent a word or phrase? Think about something that can be hard to describe. Invent a word or phrase to describe it!

One Hungry Imagination

Suzanne Collins was born in Hartford, Connecticut, in 1962, and she grew up to write one of the most successful trilogies of all time. A *trilogy* is a series of three connected books. To create hers, Collins imagined a world where children fight to the death in a televised game meant to scare the population. However, a strong young girl named Katniss Everdeen takes the games by storm, leading the people to rebel against the government. That's right, Suzanne Collins is the author of *The Hunger Games* trilogy.

The seeds of Suzanne's trilogy were most likely planted in her childhood. Suzanne's father was an Air Force officer, and her family traveled around a lot. He believed it was very important to teach his children about history and the realities of war. He took his family to battlefields and monuments, telling them about what really happened during fighting and wartime.

Despite studying dramatic writing in college, Suzanne's early career was working on children's television. For instance, she wrote for the Nickelodeon Channel. It was during this time that she began to consider writing books.

Her first successful series of books was called *The Underland Chronicles*, the first of which was published in 2003. It was called *Gregor the Overlander* and was about a boy who discovers a new world after falling through a grate in New York City. Suzanne's next book series took her from successful author to international bestseller.

The Hunger Games was first published in 2008. Suzanne Collins first created the story after seeing some televised footage of the Iraq War. It got her imagination going, and she invented a world where children fought to the death, all on national TV. One of the goals of writing the book, according to Collins, is to get kids talking about and thinking about war. She figures if we can get young people discussing wars, as she did as a child, then perhaps they can also be a part of the solutions to avoid them.

In 2009, the second book in the trilogy was released. It was called *Catching Fire*. In 2010, the final book in the series, *Mockingjay*, was published. The stories are now all being made into movies so that young people can both read and watch the heroine Katniss Everdeen as she tries to help solve the problems of her own country.

Answer the following questions about the story "One Hungry Imagination." The weights show you how hard you will need to work to find each answer.

1. In what year was Suzanne Collins born?

Ⓐ 1926   Ⓒ 1962

Ⓑ 2008   Ⓓ 2003

2. Looking at the word *trilogy*, what can you infer is the meaning of the prefix *tri-*?

Ⓐ effort   Ⓒ sequel

Ⓑ three   Ⓓ prequel

3. Based on the story, which of these statements is not true?

Ⓐ The hero of *The Hunger Games* trilogy is named Katniss.

Ⓑ Collins began her career writing drama shows for television.

Ⓒ Suzanne studied drama writing in college.

Ⓓ *Gregor the Overlander* was published in 2003.

4. What was the name of the second book from the second series of books Collins had published?

Ⓐ *The Hunger Games*   Ⓒ *Catching Fire*

Ⓑ *Gregor the Overlander*   Ⓓ *The Underland Chronicles*

On the lines below, write your own question based on "One Hungry Imagination." Circle the correct picture on the left to show the level of the question you wrote.

_____

_____

_____

_____

_____

_____

On a separate piece of paper . . .

- Write a sentence that includes the word *encouraged*.

- How do you avoid fighting with students who disagree with you? Write a list of strategies that you might use to avoid fighting with a fellow student.

How to Make Lasagna

Many of us have eaten and enjoyed baked lasagna. Dripping cheeses, bubbling sauce, and layers of flat "lasagna" noodles make us all want a second portion. The word *lasagna* can mean both the flat noodle itself or the layered pie-like meal we all know and love. There are many theories, however, about where the word came from. Some believe it is a Greek word for a kind of flat pasta. Others believe it comes from the word *loseyn*, which appeared in a 14th-century European cookbook. The cookbook described a kind of layered meal made of pasta, meat, and cheese. The noticeable difference, however, is that there were no tomatoes. After all, tomatoes didn't arrive in Europe until after Columbus got to America in 1492.

So how do you make this tasty, historical dish? Just follow these simple steps:

1. Preheat the oven (with adult supervision) to 400°F.
2. Mix together some ricotta cheese, Parmesan cheese, salt, and other Italian spices in a bowl. Put aside.
3. Prepare some slices of mozzarella cheese.
4. Open a jar of your favorite marinara sauce. A marinara sauce is a tomato-based sauce with basil. Drizzle a little on the bottom and sides of a casserole dish so the layers don't stick as they cook.
5. Put down a single layer of "no boil" lasagna noodles. They will be stiff.
6. Smear on some of the ricotta-cheese mixture on the bottom pasta layer.
7. Spoon on some more sauce.
8. Put down a layer of mozzarella cheese slices.
9. Continue layering until you run out of ingredients. End the layers by pouring the rest of the sauce over the sheet of lasagna. You can also sprinkle the top with shredded cheese to finish it off.
10. Cover the pan with aluminum foil.
11. Bake for 35–45 minutes or until done.

This is just one way to make lasagna. The possibilities are endless. You could even make the sauce yourself. That would certainly be healthier, because it would use fresher ingredients. You can also boil the pasta ahead of time rather than buy the "no boil" kind, but that will take longer.

Answer the following questions about the story "How to Make Lasagna." The weights show you how hard you will need to work to find each answer.

1. In the recipe given in the story, how is the lasagna cooked?

Ⓐ It is boiled.   Ⓒ It is fried.

Ⓑ It is baked.   Ⓓ It is microwaved.

2. Which of the following is not a type of cheese?

Ⓐ mozzarella   Ⓒ ricotta

Ⓑ marinara   Ⓓ Parmesan

3. According to the story, which of these ingredients was not found in a 14th-century loseyn?

Ⓐ pasta   Ⓒ tomato

Ⓑ meat   Ⓓ cheese

4. Based on the information given, what can you infer is the main reason to use "no boil" pasta when making lasagna?

Ⓐ It tastes better.   Ⓒ It is stiffer.

Ⓑ It cooks faster.   Ⓓ It is healthier.

On the lines below, write your own question based on "How to Make Lasagna." Circle the correct picture on the left to show the level of the question you wrote.

_____

_____

_____

_____

On a separate piece of paper . . .

• Write a sentence that includes the word *layers*.

• What do you like to cook, and why? Remember to use descriptive words to get your reader to really want to try your food!

Videoconferencing

Not too long ago, people talked on phones attached to wires. Then we moved towards cell phones that are wireless. The suffix *less* means "without." Now, we find ourselves using video-calling software more and more. What began as a gag in cartoons like "The Jetsons" has now become a reality. To videoconference someone, you can use platforms like Skype or Google. You can hook a camera up to your computer and use your computer like a phone. The difference is, of course, that you can actually see the person you are calling. In some cases, you can type in information, too. For example, let's say you want to talk to your friend and ask where you should meet at the museum. Your buddy can see you, talk to you, and text you a quick link to the museum map so that you can discuss where to meet.

However, with this new technology come different rules of netiquette. "Netiquette" is the accepted word for behavior online. It combines *net*, as in "Internet" with *etiquette*. Netiquette is, therefore, the expected manners that everyone should use when they are communicating over the Internet. Here are some netiquette rules to remember when communicating during a videoconference:

1. **Ask first, before you ring**. If you see someone online, send him or her a chat box first with the phrase, "Are you available to videoconference?" Don't just call.

2. **Be an engaged audience**. Show that you are listening. Talk directly to the camera, not your own image on the screen. It's important to focus your attention on the person with whom you are speaking. Don't get distracted or start talking or laughing with someone off-camera.

3. **Don't distract those who are video conferencing**. Even if you aren't involved in the call, don't distract those who are. Just as it is rude to ask questions of someone on the phone, it is also rude to try to get someone's attention when that person is videoconferencing on the computer.

4. **Be forgiving of technical *glitches***. Whenever you use technology, remember that things can go wrong. Be patient. When things do go wrong, be flexible. Maybe you should even resort to talking on the phone instead!

Answer the following questions about the story "Videoconferencing." The weights show you how hard you will need to work to find each answer.

1. Based on the information provided by the passage, what word might mean "without taste"?

    Ⓐ flavorful   Ⓒ flavorsome

    Ⓑ flavor-filled   Ⓓ flavorless

2. Based on the passage, what is another example of good netiquette?

    Ⓐ making sure you don't type with all capital letters

    Ⓑ posting pictures of people on the Internet without asking their permission

    Ⓒ spreading rumors over the Internet

    Ⓓ sending your friend's private e-mail to everyone you know

3. What makes videoconferencing different than making a traditional phone call?

    Ⓐ You can talk to a friend.   Ⓒ You can see a friend.

    Ⓑ You can make plans with a friend.   Ⓓ You can text a friend.

4. Based on the way it is used in the story, what seems to be the meaning of the word *glitches*?

    Ⓐ things that go wrong   Ⓒ things that are exciting

    Ⓑ things that run perfectly smoothly   Ⓓ things that are boring

On the lines below, write your own question based on "Videoconferencing." Circle the correct picture on the left to show the level of the question you wrote.

_____

_____

_____

_____

On a separate piece of paper . . .

• Write a sentence that includes the word *rude*.

• Imagine that you could videoconference with anyone in history. Write a page-long dialogue with that historic figure telling them about how you can use videoconferencing.

Growing an Edible Garden

Many gardens are beautiful to look at. Some even attract certain creatures like hummingbird or butterflies. Perhaps, however, the most useful gardens of them all are edible gardens. With this type of garden, you can eat what you grow.

An edible garden might cost extra money to set up, but it also might save you money in the long run. That's because you eat what you grow, and this will save you money at the grocery store.

The three most important elements for any garden are soil, light, and water. So thinking about those elements is a great place to start planning your first edible garden.

1. **Soil**—When you pick a place for your plants, make sure that the soil is deep and rich in color. Soil with these characteristics tends to be healthy and rich in the types of minerals that plants need. The presence of worms is one good indication of healthy soil. It seems that if the soil is suitable for worms in your dirt, it might also be good for plants.

2. **Light**—The plants need enough light on their leaves so that they may absorb the energy from the sun. Most edible plants need areas of "full sun." That phrase actually means that the location needs to be in direct sunlight for approximately six hours or so each day.

3. **Water**—Of course, plants also need water, or they will dry up and die. It can be a little tricky to figure out how much water to use, but a little trial-and-error won't hurt anything. Try watering once a day and see how the plants are doing. If they need more, they will tell you because they will become a little dry. If you have watered your plants too much, their leaves will turn a little yellow.

The next step in starting an edible garden is planning what to plant. There are some great and easy-growing options out there. For instance, during the summer months, you can grow the following:

- Herbs: basil (to make pesto sauce), cilantro (to put into salsa)
- Veggies: peppers (for flavoring), squash (for a great side dish)
- Fruit: strawberries, blueberries

Answer the following questions about the story "Growing an Edible Garden." The weights show you how hard you will need to work to find each answer.

1. If something is edible, then it _____.

   Ⓐ is always full of minerals.   Ⓒ is suitable for worms.

   Ⓑ can be eaten.   Ⓓ can be sipped.

2. What are the three most important elements to think about when gardening?

   Ⓐ soil, water, ice   Ⓒ light, minerals, heat

   Ⓑ water, light, air   Ⓓ soil, light, water

3. The second paragraph includes the phrase "in the long run." Which word could best be substituted for this phrase?

   Ⓐ "eventually"   Ⓒ "quickly"

   Ⓑ "immediately"   Ⓓ "never"

4. The paragraph about water includes the phrase, "If they need more, they will tell you." Who are the "they" that the author is referring to?

   Ⓐ the gardeners

   Ⓑ the worms

   Ⓒ the plants

   Ⓓ the grocery clerks

On the lines below, write your own question based on "Growing an Edible Garden." Circle the correct picture on the left to show the level of the question you wrote.

_____

_____

_____

_____

_____

On a separate piece of paper . . .

- Write a sentence that includes the word *approximately*.
- If you were growing a vegetable garden, what would you grow the most of and why?

How Your Keyboard Works

Once upon a time, there was a device called a typewriter. The typewriter had a keyboard that allowed the user to write onto a piece of paper. The user would hit the key with the letter, and then a little part with the letter on it would strike the paper, causing the ink to create the image on the paper. Today's keyboards look very different, but they do much the same thing.

Computer keyboards are digital. A user first clicks the key, and the button sends a signal to the computer to type a particular letter. But how does that work exactly? Keyboards are known as input devices. They put information into something else. In fact, inside a keyboard is another kind of computer. If you were to take your keyboard apart — not recommended! — you would find circuitry similar to many more complex computers.

Underneath each key is a broken circuit. By tapping the key — let's say the letter "B" — a user completes the circuit, and a signal is sent that represents that key. So when you lean on the "B" key by accident, the computer thinks you were tapping "B" over and over again because you have fit the circuit back together.

But that's not all that's happening. After you click the "B" key, and after the circuit is completed, then the computer has to translate that signal to the letter you see on the screen in front of you. That's done in the computer map that has read-only memory, or ROM. A character map is like a glossary for the computer to look up what different signals mean. The signal goes through the computer map, and out pops a B on the monitor. The character map also translates combinations of keys. If you hold down "Shift" and the number "1," out pops an exclamation mark.

A keyboard is an amazing translator. It is able to translate what you press into what you see.

Answer the following questions about the story "How Your Keyboard Works." The weights show you how hard you will need to work to find each answer.

1. Based on the passage, what similar device was used before the computer keyboard?

   Ⓐ pen and paper   Ⓒ typewriter

   Ⓑ telegraph   Ⓓ phonograph

2. What does ROM stand for?

   Ⓐ "read-only memory"   Ⓒ "read-on top of memory"

   Ⓑ "writeable-only memory"   Ⓓ "read-only memoir"

3. Which of these is an input device?

   Ⓐ monitor   Ⓒ circuit

   Ⓑ keyboard   Ⓓ glossary

4. Based on the description given in the passage, which tool does a typewriter key most act like when it puts ink on paper?

   Ⓐ screwdriver

   Ⓑ wrench

   Ⓒ tape measure

   Ⓓ hammer

On the lines below, write your own question based on "How Your Keyboard Works." Circle the correct picture on the left to show the level of the question you wrote.

_____

_____

_____

_____

On a separate piece of paper . . .

- Write a sentence that includes the word *combinations*.

- Do you think the keyboard you use is the best it can be? How would you redesign or reorder the keys to type faster and more efficiently?

How to Craft a Quiz

It's possible that you have thought that only your teacher can create quizzes to administer to you. However, it's also really powerful to make your own assessments. In fact, you can really help out your friends by creating quizzes for them to take on a subject. By creating your own questions, you are, in fact, helping facts to stick in your brain. Sure, responding to questions helps you remember answers, but some would argue that developing the questions yourself does it even more. So give it a try!

Here are some things to think about as you develop your quiz:

1. **Mix up your kinds of questions**. There are many kinds of formats you can use when developing questions for your quizzes. Mixing up your format keeps your audience interested. Here are some different kinds of formats to choose from:

   - **Essay** – Have your reader write a long response.

   - **Multiple Choice** – Have your reader choose from a series of choices.

   - **True/False** – Have your reader choose from only two choices.

   - **Short Answer** – Have your reader write a short response.

   - **Rank Order** – Have your reader rank a list (for example, "1" being best and "5" being worst) to give their opinion on a topic.

2. **Level your questions**. Create some questions that are easy and some that are more challenging. Create some questions that ask the reader to recall a fact. This would be a basic question. Then, create some questions that ask a reader to compare or contrast two facts, which would be a more complex question.

By creating an assessment that uses different formats of questions and different levels of questions, you are bound to recall the material really well. After all, as Benjamin Franklin once said, "Tell me and I forget, teach me and I may remember, involve me and I learn."

Answer the following questions about the story "How to Craft a Quiz." The weights show you how hard you will need to work to find each answer.

1. Which of these words means something different from the other words?

    Ⓐ quizzes   Ⓒ levels

    Ⓑ assessments   Ⓓ tests

2. Which question format might someone use to rate his or her opinion on a scale of 1 to 10?

    Ⓐ multiple choice   Ⓒ true/false

    Ⓑ short answer   Ⓓ rank order

3. Which word could not be used as a synonym for the word *craft* in the title of this story?

    Ⓐ arts   Ⓒ create

    Ⓑ fashion   Ⓓ construct

4. According to Benjamin Franklin, how do you best learn?

    Ⓐ by being told something

    Ⓑ by being taught something

    Ⓒ by being involved in creating something

    Ⓓ by being quizzed about something

On the lines below, write your own question based on "How to Craft a Quiz." Circle the correct picture on the left to show the level of the question you wrote.

_____

_____

_____

_____

On a separate piece of paper . . .

- Write a sentence that includes the word *assessment*.

- As you've been going through this workbook, you have been developing questions on each selection. Look back at all of your questions and compile them into a quiz for a classmate.

Answer Key

Accept appropriate responses for the final three entries on the question-and-answer pages.

The Library of Alexandria (page 11)
1. D   3. D
2. A   4. B

The First Passengers (page 13)
1. B   3. D
2. A   4. C

Patterns All Around Us (page 15)
1. A   3. C
2. B   4. C

21st-Century Energy Sources (page 17)
1. A   3. C
2. C   4. A

Sci-Fi Influences Science (page 19)
1. B   3. D
2. C   4. D

At the Same Time in History (page 21)
1. A   3. D
2. C   4. B

Fiction Made From Facts (page 23)
1. D   3. D
2. D   4. B

A Remarkable Find (page 25)
1. C   3. B
2. D   4. B

An Enormous Enigma (page 27)
1. D   3. B
2. D   4. B

Multicultural Holidays (page 29)
1. D   3. D
2. A   4. A

The Man Behind the Movies (page 31)
1. C   3. C
2. A   4. D

Science and Art Combined (page 33)
1. B   3. B
2. C   4. B

His Words Live On (page 35)
1. D   3. A
2. B   4. D

One Hungry Imagination (page 37)
1. C   3. B
2. B   4. C

How to Make Lasagna (page 39)
1. B   3. C
2. B   4. B

Videoconferencing (page 41)
1. D   3. C
2. A   4. A

Growing an Edible Garden (page 43)
1. B   3. A
2. D   4. C

How Your Keyboard Works (page 45)
1. C   3. B
2. A   4. D

How to Craft a Quiz (page 47)
1. C   3. A
2. D   4. C